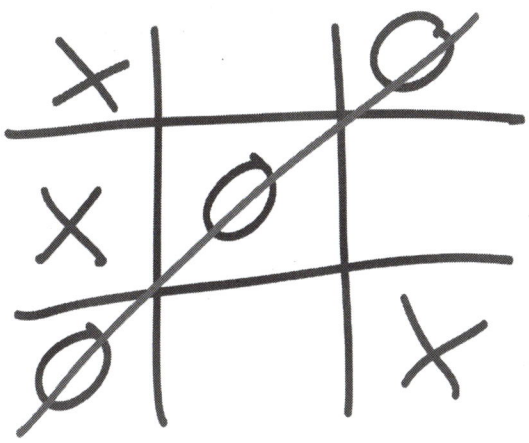

650 | Lessons Learned

Edited by Edward McCann

650 | WHERE WRITERS READ

Founder / Editor • Edward McCann
Executive Producer • Richard Kollath
Literary Ombudsman / Senior Editor • Steven Lewis
Chief of Operations • Jane Kaupp
Technical Advisor • Conrad Trautmann
Technical Advisor • Stephen Kaupp
Director of Communications • Gretchen Reed
Director of Photography • Kevin O'Connor
Videography/Photography • Sara Caldwell
Chief Audio Engineer • Jesse Chason
Copy Editor • Shelley Sadler Kenney
Copy Editor • Kathleen Stanley
Graphic Designer • Diane Fokas

Production Assistants
Robert and Lynn Dennison, Diane Fokas, Mackenzie Meeks,
Jackie Mercurio, Jessica Rao, and Brian Reagher

Advisory Committee
Rachel Aydt, Laura Shaine Cunningham, Angela Davis-Gardner,
Joseph Goodrich, Steven Lewis, David Masello, Honor Molloy,
Irene O'Garden, John Pielmeier, James Russek,
Angela Derecas Taylor, Julie Trelstad, and Gretchen Reed

650 | **Lessons Learned**
Copyright © 2018 Edward McCann
All rights reserved
ISBN 978-1-7326707-4-7
Read650.com

> "The quickest way to become an old dog
> is to stop learning new tricks."
> —*John Rooney*

ABOUT 650

Learning never stops. It begins before birth, in the earliest glimmer of consciousness, when certain sounds or movements or even tastes begin to soothe or agitate the new human growing—and learning—within. Real learning begins when we enter the world, with our lives a cinematic fast forward through learning to walk and tie shoelaces, to a first bus ride, algebra test, driving test, and swim test; through learning to cook and dance and play an instrument, from being hired and fired and falling in and out of love—the gamut of lived human experiences, all of which, in their own way, teach us things. They are rites of passage, or life lessons.

Life lessons are embedded throughout the anthology you hold in your hands—stories performed before an audience at Vassar College on how to handle difficult questions, or read music, or respond to racism, or cope with trauma and loss, or keep a marriage alive.

Read650 is a celebration of writing and the spoken word—a literary forum featuring two-page, 650-word personal stories that can be performed in five minutes. Our events at theaters, colleges, and libraries around the country are organized around single, broad topics that invite a range of expression, and recorded performances are added to a digital archive of writers reading their work aloud. The writers and their work receive additional exposure through podcasts, broadcasts, our YouTube channel, and in these printed volumes.

Read 650 features graduate students and grandparents, first-timers and bestsellers. It's all about the writing, with an emphasis on craft. It's about the choice of one word over another, about the shape of sentences and paragraphs, the arc of a narrative, the poetry of a unique literary voice. If you love language and enjoy a good story, you've come to the right place. To submit your work or attend our shows, visit our website or Facebook page, and join our mailing list.

Tell your friends about us, and **spread the word about the spoken word.**

Ed McCann

Edward McCann, Founder / Editor

READ650.COM
FACEBOOK.COM/READ650

CONTENTS

Dearly Beloved • Cari Pattison / 1

Doctor's Orders • Jack O'Connell / 5

Dave McKenna was a Legend • Karen Dukess / 9

On the Moors • John Gredler / 13

Camp Cook • Sarah Bracey White / 17

First Love • Betty MacDonald / 21

The Happening • Margarita Meyendorff / 25

Girlfriends • John Pielmeier / 29

What He Knew • Kathy Curto / 33

Life Lessons • Annabel Monaghan / 37

The "M" Word • Tracey Doolittle McNally / 41

The Greenest Shade of Green • Anna Paret / 45

Not My Father's Cadillac • Steven Lewis / 49

Requiem • Edward McCann / 53

Acknowledgements / 57

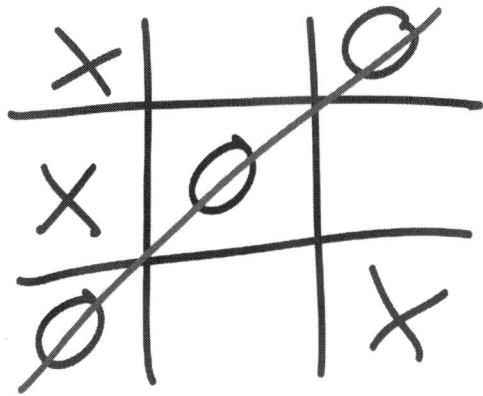

650 | Lessons Learned

Edited by Edward McCann

CARI PATTISON

The Reverend Cari Pattison has served ten years as the associate minister at The Reformed Church of Bronxville, New York. In addition to ministry, Cari trained as a jazzercise, yoga, barre, and Pilates instructor, seeking to inspire people in body and spirit. Originally from Kansas City, Cari studied English and Art at Kalamazoo College in Michigan and earned her Masters of Divinity at Princeton Theological Seminary in New Jersey. She previously taught eighth-grade English in Missouri, and served a variety of churches and hospitals in Kansas, Kenya, and New Jersey. Cari has blogged for the *Huffington Post*, illustrated the children's book *ABC: Sing with Me*, and is a 2015 recipient of the Kathryn Gurfein Fellowship at The Writing Institute of Sarah Lawrence College.

DEARLY BELOVED
Cari Pattison

I get invited to a lot of weddings. Not for my wide circle of friends nor my charm as a guest, and not for my connections to yacht clubs or my fashion sense—unless you're into black wool.

I go to so many weddings because I officiate them. As an ordained minister, I show the groom how to place the ring on his bride without jamming her finger, and store tissues in my folder for unexpected tears during the vows. I crafted a "Midsummer Night's Dream" wedding for one couple, and for another I agreed to let them include in their ceremony: "I love being naughty with you." I'm a sucker for a good love story.

But the minister role can be a delicate one. I've sat across from two twenty-somethings and watched the girl's face fall when her fiancé said he didn't believe in marriage. I advised them to perhaps postpone the wedding. The bride called the next day to fire me so they could find an officiant who would be "more supportive."

Another summer a couple rented our sanctuary for their large-scale wedding and all went well until their church hierarchy told them female pastors were not allowed. "That's inconvenient," I said, "since the male clergy are away, and at least one of us has to co-officiate." The bride consulted their bishop, and called to say, "Turns out you can't do any minister parts, but you've been granted special permission to light the unity candle."

Unity is not my specialty. I officiated my first-ever wedding the same week I told my husband I wanted to separate. In a cruel bit of irony, my nickname for him was "Dearly Beloved," or "Dearly" for short.

After my marriage ended, I flew out to Ohio to officiate my brother George's wedding. Some of my relatives had been silent since my divorce, and I pictured standing before disapproving family members who prided themselves on "making marriage work." When I shared my fears, my mom said, "You don't have to officiate."

But memories of George flashed through my mind: the three-year-old circling the basement in a big wheel, the six-year-old shooting hoops in the driveway, the ten-year-old jumping off the diving board—always saying, "Did you see that, Cari? How 'bout me? The Number 1! How 'bout me? The MVP!" I babysat him, played board games with him, and built bed-tents with him. No one but me would pronounce him somebody's husband.

At the hotel in Columbus, I went outside to review my notes. My dad's friend Dave stepped out for a cigarette. "Can I have one?" I said. Knowing I don't smoke, he laughed, "How's it going, Preacher?" A former Air Force technician with thick white hair, Dave had married my mom's friend after she caught his eye wearing leopard-print pants. It was his third marriage.

I confessed my doubts: "I don't exactly feel like the love-and-marriage guru right now." Dave looked me square in the eye and said, "You've got this."

An hour later at the chapel, there was George, standing in front of me in gray suit and green-and-navy-striped tie, shifting his weight from left to right. The kid brother I remembered was now a man I loved so fiercely it was all I could do to keep the tears behind my eyes from spilling out into the pews.

And there behind that wooden podium, I let go my tale of woe, my fears of what anyone thought, because there was a love story to tell, and I got to be the one to tell it—to bless and pray and endorse and point to the source of all love—the One who's there even when the story changes.

I looked out and took a deep breath.

"Dearly Beloved ... " I began.

I smiled at my brother, the MVP, and knew I was right where I needed to be.

JACK O'CONNELL

Jack O'Connell is a New York City native presently living on Long Island with his wife, Margaret. He is a working actor with extensive film credits including *Doubt, Big Night, Inside Llewyn Davis, The Paper, God's Pocket, The Quitter, Brazzaville Teenager, Everyday People, The Yards,* and others. Numerous TV credits include *Mad Men, Nurse Jackie,* and *Vinyl,* and Jack is currently seen on the Netflix hit *The Marvelous Mrs. Maisel,* playing Jerry the elevator operator. Jack is a member of Artists Without Walls.

DOCTOR'S ORDERS
Jack O'Connell

"Don't worry Mr. O'Connell. Your insurance covers it." That line alone told me the cardiac rehab service was overpriced. It was late winter, 2001, I was mending from heart by-pass surgery and shopping for a prescribed exercise rehab facility. I was told about measured walks around a track at this state-of-the-art facility. And walking was something I loved to do and the distance prescribed was not a factor. But yes, it was overpriced. I figured I could do this on my own.

A walk around the West End of Jones Beach was three miles. While measuring the distance the next day I came upon a notice, "Seasonal Help Wanted," part-time laborer at $6.91 per hour. I was hired and told the starting date would be mid-April. On April 16, my boss Quinnie handed me a hat, gloves, and a pick stick and told me to go out and collect anything that didn't grow. Along the Bay, past the Coast Guard Station beside the inlet and back. Mostly plastic, bottles, tackle, and many deflated party balloons. Loved the freedom of walking alone, fresh air, flora blooming in the brush, and the quiet. A communion with nature, my own rehab.

Most employees during summer months were high school or college students. I was known as "The Old Guy" or "The Crazy Old Guy" when I suggested they change the bucket water before mopping the rest rooms each morning.

After a while I never spoke much to anyone and kept to myself. Things seemed to work better that way. I was there to regain my physical strength, not make friends with kids young enough to be my children At lunch I would sit in my car with sandwich and water. Radio, "Music of Your Life" on a local AM station. "And now the No. 1 tune of 1955, Perez Prado's "Cherry Pink and Apple Blossom White." As the trumpet slid down and then up before the melody, my eyes closed, and my thoughts would drift back to Rockaway in the summer of '55. My mother handing me an egg salad sandwich wrapped in wax paper and a cheese glass of grape Kool Aid. Then thinking that I sit here twenty miles to the East, looking at the same ocean, listening to same tune, trying to preserve that Mambo spirit in my heart.

My summer job was just what the doctor ordered.

My last day would be September 13, a Thursday. On Friday I was scheduled to start rehearsals for the Arthur Miller play "All My Sons." We were supposed to open on October 25 at The Hampton Theatre Co. out in Quogue. This job was actually a good physical warm-up for my role.

On the morning of Tuesday, September 11, with my helper Robert next to me in the cab of our pick-up, we set out to pick the beach. While driving along the high tide line where much of the debris lines up, Don Imus's voice came crackling through our walkie talkie. Imus said a plane had crashed into the World Trade Center. My first thoughts were this is a terrible radio prank, but soon learned differently.

A feeling came over me similar to the morning I was wheeled onto an elevator to go up to the operating room. Cleanly scrubbed, things were out of my hands now. Suddenly I prayed that morning at the Beach, as I did on the elevator at St. Francis Hospital.

My heart ached for the victims. For their families. For all of us. And I knew that morning what my young co-workers were to find: that we are helpless at times, and at times we are the helpers.

KAREN DUKESS

Karen Dukess is the author of the novel *The Last Book Party*, to be published in July 2019 by Henry Holt & Co. She has been a tour guide in the former Soviet Union, a newspaper reporter at the *St. Petersburg Times* in Florida, and the founding features editor of *The Moscow Times* in Russia. She has written book reviews for *USAToday* and blogged about raising teen-aged boys at theblunderyears.com and the *Huffington Post*. Her narrative non-fiction has appeared in *Intima* (Columbia University) and her short story, "Fancy Hat," appeared in the 2017 issue of the *Westchester Review*. She is a speechwriter at UN Development Programme and is a member of the Terzo Piano writer's group. She lives in Pelham, New York.

DAVE McKENNA WAS A LEGEND
Karen Dukess

I was in my sophomore year at college when I got a surprise phone call from my father. "Want a date for Friday night?" he asked. The jazz pianist Dave McKenna would be playing at a club in Providence and my father had two tickets. He would drive up from New York and be outside my dorm at 6.

Dave McKenna was "a legend," my father had often told me.

"Just listen to his unusual sense of time," he'd said a few months earlier, after getting a new McKenna album. "Do you hear it?"

"Yup," I said, and waited for that inevitable moment when he would lift the needle from the LP and place it down ever so carefully so I could hear a particular bridge again.

Glenn Miller, Duke Ellington, Benny Goodman, Bob Wilber - my father loved them all. I heard them all, and I heard about them all, without really listening. My father's music was ancient and musty, with songs you could sing along to only by muttering "bah-bah-baa" or "do-dah-do-do," which he never hesitated to do when one of his favorites came on the car radio.

At six o'clock, just as promised, Dad rolled up to my dorm. The jazz club was small and dark; the audience old. Slumped at the piano, McKenna was a wide-shouldered guy in a suit and tie. With thinning hair, he looked more like a washed-out insurance salesman than a legendary jazz pianist.

McKenna was impressive on the piano, but I found the music slippery, difficult to latch onto, endless. My father was enraptured.

After the second set, my Dad walked up to the piano to talk to Mr. McKenna and buy an album for me. He beamed when his idol smiled my way and autographed the cover. I thanked them both for the album, which I later slid onto a shelf in my dorm room, and never played.

Two years ago, decades after I lost track of that neglected album, my son Johnny started playing piano. His repertoire was typical for a young teenager: a lot of Billy Joel and some Beatles. It was not my father's favorite music, but he loved to listen to Johnny play anyway – even when he got too weak to come downstairs to sit by the piano.

And then this autumn, a few months after my father died, Johnny's piano teacher taught him some jazz tunes—Miles Davis and Thelonius Monk—and introduced him to Duke Ellington, Art Tatum and Dick Hyman. Johnny practiced jazz chords and riffs, learned blues scales, and started improvising, the music flowing from him with a seemingly effortless joy.

One evening, while Johnny was playing the piano and I was making dinner in the kitchen, I realized: I know this music; this is the soundtrack of my childhood.

I followed the intertwining strands of melody, and stayed with the songs as they rose and wandered and came back around again. The rhythms were intoxicating, the bridges artful. How had I not heard any of it before? Why had my father's passion for jazz—so constant and true—touched me only when he was gone?

I read in the paper recently that scientists have recorded the sound of two black holes colliding a billion light years away, and that this is evidence that space and time are interwoven, as Einstein said. I don't understand this, but I would like to believe that time rippling and bending means that when Johnny and I listen to one of my father's old Dave McKenna recordings, my father is hearing it, too, that we are all in the exact same moment, happy and slightly astonished, as the melody, and the technique, and the magic take us away.

JOHN GREDLER

John Gredler, poet and memoirist, is a frequent contributor to 650 who's been writing in notebooks and journals for most of his adult life. He honed his craft at the Writing Institute at Sarah Lawrence College, Bella Villa Writers, 125, and the Terzo Piano Workshops. A recipient of the 2014 Kathryn Gurfein Fellowship from The Writing Institute at Sarah Lawrence College, John's work has been published in *Atticus Review, Fictionique, Narratively, Dan's Papers, Westchester Review,* and *Talking Writing*. John lives and writes in Tuckahoe, New York.

ON THE MOORS
John Gredler

For the first few weeks every time I called Terri, she answered the phone already sobbing. She was an au pair and had gone home to England for Christmas. On the return trip, when she arrived at JFK customs agents put her on the next flight back to London. She had violated her work visa. Deported. Ten years.

I met with an immigration lawyer who told me the only solution would be to marry. Even if we could convince the State Department it was real it might take months before she would be able to return.

I was in love with her. I told her I would marry her. By the time we got all the details and paperwork sorted out it was March.

When I got off the plane at Gatwick I saw Terri bouncing nervously on tiptoe searching the crowd. She spotted me, ran over and held me tight, knocking me off balance. On the train up north she was constantly fidgeting, fixing her hair, inspecting her fingernails, checking her makeup. I was curiously calm, willing to do this for her.

That night I very much wanted to be with Terri as we had been back in New York. She was reticent, trying to put me off. When she eventually gave in it was like it had been with us before, but different. I could feel a change in her.

The day we were to get married Terri was so anxious she had to take some Valium. That morning she'd done her hair up into a single braid running down her back. Her skin was shining, like porcelain. We drove to the town hall where a tall pale solicitor read the vows. When he asked Terri if she took me as her husband she hesitated, then gave a nervous laugh before managing to say "I do."

We went the next day to the Lake District for our 'honeymoon'. At the inn we were staying she became peevish and disagreeable, picking at me over small things, criticizing my clothing and my hair.

We booked a boat tour of the lake. I took her picture, hair frizzed by the rain, her smile a brilliant facade, her eyes wondrous empty things with gray crescents underneath.

When I told her I'd like to see the Bronte Parsonage she surprised me, seeming excited by the idea. A road trip to take us away from that sodden place.

The parsonage itself a foreboding stone structure, the exhibits disappointing. I walked outside, coming to the cemetery with it's big oak trees, branches bare of leaves, studded with black crows arguing.

Looking past the uneven rows of gravestones to the empty wind swept moors, I understood where the Bronte sisters found inspiration.

The memory came to me of the time we were in my car on the Upper West Side, both a little bit "looped' as Terri would say, and very hot for each other. I pulled down one of those long blocks between 11th Avenue and the West Side Highway parking in the darkest spot I could find. We went at each other. I was surprised and excited when she peeled off her dress like a shirt and tossed it into the back seat. In a moment she was naked, pulling me to her.

After we finished, dripping sweat, the windows of the car clouded with condensation, I lay with my head on her breast breathing in the thick sweet aroma that came from us, listening to the sound of her heart beating through her damp skin.

The deep metallic chortle of a group of crows on a branch nearby shook me from my reverie, a gust of wind tearing them from their perch, wheeling them up above the cemetery and out over the moors, the rest of the flock following. I stood watching until they were only black specks shot across the slate colored clouds, vanishing into the horizon.

SARAH BRACEY WHITE

Sarah Bracey White is a writer, teacher, and arts consultant. A graduate of Morgan State University and the University of Maryland, she's a former Inaugural Fellow at the Purchase College Writers Center. Published work includes *Primary Lessons: A Memoir The Wanderlust: A South Carolina Folk Tale,* and *Feelings Brought to Surface,* a poetry collection. Her memoir piece, *Freedom Summer,* was included in the anthologies *Children of the Dream, and Dreaming in Color, Living in Black and White.* Her essays appear in *Aunties: 35 Writers Celebrate Their Other Mothers, Gardening on a Deeper Level,* and *Heartscapes: True Stories of Remembered Loves.* Her essays have appeared in *The New York Times, The Baltimore Afro American Newspaper,* the *Scarsdale Inquirer,* and the *Journal News.* She and her husband live in Ossining, New York.

CAMP COOK
Sarah Bracey White

In 1963, days after my graduation from a segregated South Carolina high school, I boarded a train for Ely, Vermont, where, even though I knew little about cooking, I was to be the head cook's assistant at an exclusive girls' camp nestled on the shores of Lake Fairlee. I dreamed of learning to swim in the beautiful lake pictured in the camp's brochure. Upon arrival, however, Camp Beenadeewin's owner told us that the kitchen help was not allowed to go near Lake Fairlee. We also were told not to associate with the white campers, and to address each one as "Miss" during all encounters in the dining hall. Up north, it seemed, segregation was a matter of class and skin color.

I was incensed and wanted to bolt; but, I had no way to get home, and no home to return to. My mother had died a few months earlier and I'd had no contact with my absentee father for years. Beenadeewin was to have been my interim home until I entered Morgan State College that fall. The camp's offer of room, board, a round-trip train ticket, and $300, in exchange for two months' labor, no longer seemed fair; but, I accepted my fate.

Mrs. Lee, the head cook, six other teen-aged girls and I quickly settled into the routine of preparing and serving home-cooked meals for 150 people, three times a day, six-and-a-half-days a week. It was cold and dark each morning as I made my way through the pine-scented forest to the kitchen where I stirred huge vats of Maypo, loaded slices of white bread onto an industrial-sized toaster, then buttered and pressed each slice into a plate of cinnamon sugar. Under Mrs. Lee's tutelage, I learned to make, and enjoy, delicacies like sugar cookies, clover-leaf dinner rolls, and smooth, brown gravy for pot roasts.

Despite my anger about the restrictions at camp, I was shamelessly curious about the campers. Never before had I been in such close proximity to so many white people my age. From my side of the kitchen counter, it grew easier day-by-day to eavesdrop on their conversations as they grew used to our brown presence and we became about as insignificant as the pine trees.

I soon learned that white skin brought no solace from money problems, didn't ensure smooth boy/girl relationships, or prevent sadness and heartache. They had the same problems I had! I also learned that having two parents at home didn't always make a happy family.

Every Sunday afternoon, the resident handyman took the seven of us sightseeing in the camp's old, woody station wagon. I marveled at the beauty of the Vermont countryside, and the quaintness of its villages. I surmised from the stares that our little group always drew that no other colored people had ever lived in, or visited, the state of Vermont. An overwhelming sense of being different, and unwelcome, permeated my entire experience. I vowed that once I left Vermont, I would never return.

The last Sunday afternoon before camp ended, instead of joining the weekly tour, I made a pilgrimage through the pine forests to the forbidden Lake Fairlee. As I looked out over the vast, mirror-like expanse, I grew angry. What right did white people have to bar me from something God made? Since they thought my skin would contaminate their lake, I decided to do something that really would. I stepped into the water, squatted, and peed.

BETTY MacDONALD

Writer/actor **Betty MacDonald** contributed to the writing of and performed in TMI's *What To Expect When You're Not Expecting*. Her essay *Before Roe v Wade* appears in the anthology *Get Out of My Crotch*, published by Cherry Bomb Press. Betty especially enjoys reading aloud and frequently reads her work at spoken word events throughout the Hudson River Valley. Following her early career as a continuity writer and radio personality, Betty freelanced for many years as a travel writer. For the last twenty-six years, storytelling has influenced her work as a performer with Community Playback Theatre, a regional improvisational acting company. Her memoir, *Basking In The Glow Of Her Golden Years*, is nearly complete.

FIRST LOVE
Betty MacDonald

Because he slips into her bed at night after he comes home from a date. Because he is insistent, she lets him. She lets him because she adores her brother with the intensity of a little sister. She knows it's wrong.

She longs for his approval. After years of ignoring her and putting her down, he's focused on her. He wants her. She wants to be special.

She tries to stop but the lure to please him overrides her resistance.

She stops him from "going all the way." They do everything else. Her boundaries battered and porous from her father's incessant assault ... she wonders if her brother is also the object of unwanted touching from their father.

When she is nine and her brother thirteen, they are the same height. Their mother's nightmare: a shrimp of a son and a giant daughter. At eleven and fifteen, they look like twins, twin nymphs. He is tall by then and handsome. They're so young, so fresh bodied, like star crossed lovers ... like loving brother and sister god and goddess in a Greek myth ... in a Celtic myth ... in a Viking myth. So much alike, could you tell them apart when they were entwined in each other's arms?

On a visit to their uncle a few years later, their uncle remarks, "You act as if you are his wife, not his sister."

Is that just a snarky remark? Does he know?

Does he know her fantasy dream-like locked away secret, not to be revealed, not to be acted upon: Her lover, a male version of herself, her exact counterpart. No one can know.

Fortunately what they share is forbidden. Without that inhibition, she would have lost herself in him.

On the one hand, she is dragged down by the weight of the secret ... the forbidden-ness of it.

On the other, she loves their star crossedness, love-that-can-never-be, tragic story of it. Willingly, she promises herself she will welcome letting go when he commits to someone else.

When it ends, it has gone on for ten years.

They never speak about it. They don't even have a name for it. Later on she tells friends, therapists, a twelve-step group, anyone who will listen. He tells no one. He doesn't admit it to himself.

In his early sixties, he is diagnosed with Alzheimer's. When she visits him at his nursing home, he thinks it is 1950, and that they are in their teens.

On these rare visits, they sit side by side, holding hands, saying little. She could say she feels their souls touching, she could say there is an electric current, but it's not like that. A powerful feeling like no other courses from his hand into hers. She weeps whenever she remembers the feeling of their hands pressed together.

He was mean when they were kids. He never forgave her for

reducing his lofty privileged only-child status to that of big brother. She had loved him unconditionally, in spite of his cutting her hair off, sawing her tricycle in half, burning the end of her nose with the cigarette lighter in the new Chevrolet. Her cousin asks, "Do you remember when he held you down with a pillow over your face till you passed out?" She doesn't.

At seventy-eight the Alzheimer's has advanced. She is the only person he recognizes.

He has broken his hip. The hip has healed. But he can't walk. He's forgotten how. It's near the end.

She sits pressing herself into him as close as she can. She holds his hand firmly. She wills the closeness to direct her words to what shreds of memory he has left.

"I forgive you." She says. "Do you understand?"

"Yes," he says nodding, "I think I do!"

MARGARITA MEYENDORFF

Margarita Meyendorff (Mourka) is the author of the memoir *DP: Displaced Person*. The daughter of a Russian Baron, she was born displaced, far from the opulence of Imperial Russia that was her birthright. A series of wars destroyed this privileged existence, and Margarita's life became a series of extraordinary moves. She has performed as an actress, dancer, musician, and storyteller at venues throughout the United States and in Europe.

THE HAPPENING
Margarita Meyendorr

"There's a Halloween costume party tonight up in Palenville," Lynn said on the phone. "I think we should go. It's supposed to be a 'happening.' Rumor has it that the all-male band is performing naked."

"But what are we wearing? Do you have a costume? I don't have a costume." I said.

"No worries. I'll meet you at your house in an hour. Find something to put on," she said. "It will be fun." And the phone clicked.

Leave it to Lynn, my good friend, a modern dancer and choreographer extraordinaire, to dig up this party in Palenville, a tiny village in upstate New York in the middle of nowhere. My children were with my ex-husband, and I had the night off. Why not?

As I stood loading dirty clothes into the washing machine, I glanced up at the wall of my laundry room at the single decoration—a bright red communist flag with the yellow hammer and sickle insignia in the center. A few years back, I had bought this flag in Moscow and displayed it over the washing machine to depict my daily proletariat tasks.

My inner voice whispered: "Wear it!" Could I go wrapped in a communist flag? After all, Gorbachev's Perestroika was in full effect in Russia. I dumped the dirty clothes into the washer, took down the flag, ran upstairs and stripped. I wrapped the flag around me . . . twice. The mini flag dress fit perfectly from just above my breasts to just above my knees, the hammer and sickle making a perfect design in the middle of my body. I pulled up my hair for formal flair, donned red high heels and pinned several Russian military medals to my chest. If the band was appearing naked, I could be a Russian General wearing the flag. With safety pins holding me and the flag together, I could hardly walk, much less sit or dance for fear of unraveling.

The door opened and I gasped as Lynn walked in, dressed as the ghost of Martha Graham, holding a large, lit candelabra in her black-gloved hands. Her face was white with powder, eyes outlined in heavy black, no lipstick. She was wearing a long tight black dress with a turtleneck collar and her hair was pulled back tight in a bun with chopsticks protruding. Lynn bore an uncanny resemblance to Martha anyway, but in this outfit, she embodied her. Lynn was dressed to the gills; I was half naked.

Very careful not to disturb the safety pins and chopsticks, we climbed into the car and headed for the party. We were famished because in the excitement, we had forgotten to eat. The only recourse was to stop at the drive through Burger King window at the Thruway entrance. We managed to eat our Whoppers without too much movement and continued on our way.

The party was packed with people who were on various levels of alcohol and marijuana highs. Everyone was in a tizzy, awaiting the advertised naked musicians. When four nice-looking musicians finally did appear—yes, naked with glow paint on their 'members,' the crowd roared in appreciation. From my perspective, they were a partial disappointment as they quickly hid behind their instruments—

the guitar and cello players more successfully than the saxophonist. The rest of the evening, Lynn floated through the crowd with the lit candelabra and I fussed with my communist flag mini-dress as the heavy Soviet medals were threatening to open and expose my breasts.

The next day the *Kingston Freeman* ran an article on the front page—*Nudity and Commies in Palenville* and 'named names'—a few prominent Woodstock citizens who attended. Had I known there was a right-wing reporter at the gathering, I would have let my flag slip to reveal my "left wing" breast and really given him something to write about.

JOHN PIELMEIER

John Pielmeier began his career with the play and movie *Agnes of God*. Since then, he has had three more plays mounted on Broadway and twenty-five film, television movies and miniseries produced. Most recently he has written and acted in the internationally successful limited series, *The Pillars of the Earth*, and his stage adaptation of *The Exorcist* premiered in the West End in 2017 and is bound for Broadway. His first novel, *Hook's Tale*, was published by Scribner in July 2017. In between, he has received the Humanitas Award (plus two nominations), five Writers' Guild Award nominations, a Gemini Award (plus a nomination), an Edgar Award, the Camie Award, a Christopher Award, and been nominated for the Emmy Award (three times) and the Golden Globe Award. He is married to writer Irene O'Garden and makes his home in upstate New York.

GIRLFRIENDS
John Pielmeier

Their names were Mart and Alison and they came to visit us on occasion, and once or twice we went to visit them. They were school teachers, I believe, and lived together on the top floor of an old brick house. Mart was tall and thin and wore her dark hair in a bun; Alison was shorter and red-haired and might have been the kind of woman once called "handsome." Her last name, I believe, was Douglas, which I found confusing because even though my mother referred to them as "Martin Alison" I always thought of them as "Alice and Douglas." Their names were linked as though they were one person, half female, half male, which in some ways struck ten-year-old me as not incorrect.

Nearly all of my mother's girlfriends were of the same physical mold. They were thin and wiry or square and muscular and all of them were unmarried, but for one who had several children and a mustache. Most were gym teachers, and they were all what my mother might call "outdoorsy." She first met them when she worked as a secretary for the Girl Scouts; they were leaders and administrators, and they were all very fond of her. She welcomed them when they visited with a kindness shadowed by a certain reluctance I never completely understood. I liked them; they were fun to be around and they seemed comfortable in their bodies in ways that other women weren't. They were independent, and they seemed happy.

My mother and her girlfriends spent the summers of the 1930's at a Girl Scout camp near their hometown. All were camp counsellors, and they bonded, I imagine, sitting around a campfire late at night after their young charges were in bed, talking of the girls and their pre-teen problems, and celebrating their own love of being in the great outdoors away from civilization and the tyranny of men.

My mother's boss, a woman named Billie, introduced my mother to my father, and my mother always spoke of Billie with great affection, still remembering the sorrow she suffered when Billie moved to another city and another Girl Scout office. She and Billie exchanged Christmas cards every year, and when I was grown I arranged for my mother and Billie to see each other again. I met Billie for the first time then: she was square and muscular and very outdoorsy. My mother was happy to see her, but the meeting was a little awkward: they didn't have a lot to say to each other and they never saw each other again.

Once, I remember, our next-door neighbor Georgetta referred to one of my mother's friends as a lesbian. Mother was incensed. It was as if Georgetta had accused the woman, in the paranoia of the late 1950's, of being a Russian spy. To tell the truth (in the spirit of that metaphor) all of my mother's girlfriends spoke with thick Russian accents and carried tiny spy cameras hidden in their spectacles; still, my mother denied their foreign allegiance. Even when her closest friend—a solid woman named Marian who had a contagious laugh and eyes that squinted with warmth—even when Marian moved in with another woman (an action I'm sure my mother did not approve of) my mother refused to judge her. She prayed for her, I imagine, but she always welcomed Marian gladly when the woman came to visit.

The happiest six months of my mother's life was when she served as a substitute girls' gym teacher at my high school. Years later, when my wife and I celebrated our tenth anniversary with a party and a dance, my mother spent the evening cutting a rug with a female friend of ours. "Your mother's a terrific dancer," our friend told us later. "She would have made a great lesbian."

KATHY CURTO

Kathy Curto teaches at The Writing Institute at Sarah Lawrence College, Montclair State University, and across the metropolitan area serving writers of all ages. Her work has been published in the anthology, *Listen to Your Mother: What She Said Then, What We're Saying Now,* and in publications including *Barrelhouse, Drift, Talking Writing, Junk, The Inquisitive Eater,* the *Asbury Park Press, Italian Americana, VIA-Voices in Italian Americana* and *Lumina Journal*. In 2006, she was awarded the Kathryn Gurfein Writing Fellowship at Sarah Lawrence College and also served as a 2015 to 2016 engaged teaching fellow at Montclair State. Kathy lives in Cold Spring, New York with her husband and their four children.

WHAT HE KNEW
Kathy Curto

The kids were one, three, five and six. We had no business going away with them in tow, but we were trying to stay sane and in love so we went anyway. I wanted no laundry and a meal I didn't cook. He wanted a break from work. And the kids wanted to take turns pushing a hotel elevator button. I booked a place, Mountaintop Lodge, ninety minutes away with a room that fit us all. I didn't ask about dress codes. I didn't ask about dinner seating. I didn't ask about what I now know are defined as additional charges.

In the lobby we were greeted with an onslaught of pastel sweater sets and loafers. Lots and lots of loafers. My faded jean jacket was clearly the wrong call. All eyes were on the jacket and my son, Sam. His Buzz Lightyear pajamas smelled sour and Buzz's face was stained with a blob of Yoo-hoo. Hushed remarks about the girls, too, were likely--with their uneven ponytails and the stick-on fake fingernail tips in neon colors.

I thought this was a lodge. To me, lodge meant jeans, hot dogs and s'mores. Not pressed khakis, beef Wellington and petits fours. Or afternoon tea.

"One or two keys, sir?" asked Audrey, the Reservation Specialist to my husband, Peppe.

"Two's good," he answered and signed the card that allowed us to charge our every move. Because, in addition to looking nothing like a lodge, it also didn't match my idea of what a lodge costs. There would be no cherries in the Shirley Temples for us.

We got through dinner probably because we employed Operation If You Behave as a means of survival. The kids wanted to play after so we rolled out our favorite strategy: leverage.

Earlier Audrey told us all about the "magnificent" game room. "And for your little princesses we have "spectacular" costumes!" Audrey winked, too, but looked away when she noticed two of our three princesses picking their noses.

So after dinner we went to the game room where they played dress-up and Cinderella pinball. There was even a make-your-own cotton candy machine, which is just what their already inappropriate outfits didn't need. We were done.

But as we left we noticed a dim backroom. Inside, a pool table. "When was the last time you played pool?" Peppe asked.

"College, I think," I said, realizing what that meant. We never played pool together.

"How about one game?" he nudged.

The kids were tired and sticky. But some higher power pulled them onto the fancy leather couch next to the pool table. They curled up into one another and squealed.

"No, let me watch you," I said and sat on a stool in the corner next to the sticks and chalk and ball racks. I had forgotten something about myself but when he reached for the cue stick, I was reminded.

There's a slow, smooth, deliberate manner of leaning that must happen to play pool well. He knew about that.

Then there are the ways hands and fingers and legs must work to play the game. Knew that, too.

There are the sounds. The cracks and echoes that arouse, thrill, and startle. The breaks, stunts, and tricks. There's the jukebox and there's Muddy Waters.

There are the eyes. How they watch, deepen and consider. And the way they shift up, just before the shot, maybe to see who's watching.

He looked up at me and let his cue slide forward. My eyes dwelled on his for a handful of seconds and then an epiphany: I may not have gotten off the stool but we were both playing in this game.

Still.

I gazed from him to the kids who were tangled up and almost asleep on Mountaintop's fancy leather couch.

I watched him some more.

And there, in my faded jean jacket, I was shaken and stirred.

ANNABEL MONAGHAN

Annabel Monaghan is the author of two novels for young adults, *A Girl Named Digit* and *Double Digit*. She is also the author of *Does This Volvo Make My Butt Look Big?*, a collection of essays based on her column that appears on the *Huffington Post, The Week* and *The Rye Record*. She teaches novel writing at The Writing Institute at Sarah Lawrence College and lives in Rye, New York with her husband and three sons.

LIFE LESSONS
Annabel Monaghan

The great thing about Candy Land and Chutes and Ladders is that they can be played in less than fifteen minutes and take very little mental effort. Even so, when my husband comes home from work, I can still add "played a board game with the kids" to my list of heroic accomplishments. Unfortunately, my five-year-old has developed an unhealthy interest in The Game of Life, the only game I know that is possibly more complicated than life itself.

At first I try to convince him that the little cars that lead us down life's path are there to be zoomed, and that whoever gets to the end first wins. But he isn't having it. So I figure if we were going to have to play, we'll do it right. I'll teach him a few Life lessons and get the dialogue going about the world around us. You know, actual parenting. Like on TV.

The game starts at age eighteen, and I am pleased to see that he chooses to go to college. Having made such a wise choice, he is faced with many career options after graduation. I encourage him to choose the accounting job because it comes with the possibility of the highest salary card. To my horror, he chooses to be a singer because, he claims, that's what he likes to do. Why would he spend his life doing something he doesn't like just for the money? Sigh. He's got a lot to learn.

Meandering through Life, we each stop to get married. He thinks carefully before choosing a pink peg for his spouse rather than a blue one. He buys a house, which he also chooses for its color. Later, I have to inform him that his house was robbed and that he should have bought the insurance like I told him to. Ah, an actual Life lesson!

He rejoices every time he lands on a square that gives him another baby. He fills up his car with the allotted four children and then hoards the extras in the back seat. (I have another son who likes to collect the child pegs too, but leaves them on the side of the board with his money, claiming, "I don't want those kids riding in my car." We refer to him as The Smart One.)

Life gets more complicated as you move along. He wants to know what a Pulitzer Prize is and if it comes with candy. He wants to know who has the Solution to Pollution and why anyone would want to swim across the English Channel. I can only answer one of those. At some point I find myself explaining what a stock is, then what a dividend is, and what taxes are for. And how dividends are taxed at a lower rate than ordinary income and why Warren Buffet doesn't really like that.

As Life winds down, we are laden with cash and real estate and lucky heirs, and we race toward retirement. If you can afford it you get to retire in Millionaire Estates and if you can't you're relegated to Countryside Acres. Before you enter either, you sell your house, the price of which is determined by a random spin of the wheel. Which actually sounds about right.

Life ends, and I realize I've just spent a full hour explaining to a five-year-old how life works. I wait for the applause and maybe a little confetti as we each count up our money to determine who wins. And because I chose the rejected accounting job with the coveted yellow salary card, I have the most money. I tell him with great humility that I have won and he has lost. He shakes his head and shows me his full little car, "I have the most family. I win."

I may need to rethink a few things.

TRACY DOOLITTLE McNALLY

Tracy Doolittle McNally is the former executive director of Historic Huguenot Street in New Paltz, past oresident of the Greene County Chamber of Commerce in Catskill, and past vice president of the United Way for Ulster County. Prior to her career in the nonprofit world, Tracy worked in corporate advertising as a copywriter for an international forest products company. Tracy is currently pursuing her lifelong passions of genealogy, classical ballet, and storytelling.

THE "M" WORD
Tracy Doolittle McNally

At age thirty-nine, I relocated to live and work in the Hudson Valley. Although jobs were hard to come by, I managed to land one as director of marketing and public relations at Benedictine Hospital, a Catholic hospital in Kingston. This was a big change from my previous corporate world. I knew little about hospital management and less about the Catholic Church, other than the church had tried to murder my French Huguenot ancestors in the early 1600s.

Not long after I began working, a Benedictine Sister asked me to assemble a team of four—myself included—to represent the hospital in a trivia contest to benefit another nonprofit agency. I wanted to tell the dear Sister that I'd rather poke needles in my eyes than play trivia, but since I was the new hire, I thought better of it and started searching for other players. I deliberately didn't ask any doctors to participate because I wanted to have fun and drink with the nurses. Few were game to play, and after multiple strike-outs, a colleague suggested that I approach Dr. Richard McNally. "He knows everything" she said, "music, poetry, Shakespeare, beer making, sports—and he's very nice; not like a doctor at all."

Dr. McNally and I had never met before, but on my very first day at the hospital I'd phoned him for the answer to a serious yet very awkward question posed to me by a newspaper reporter during a contentious and controversial hospital merger:

"How does a laboratory in a Catholic hospital obtain sperm for fertility testing if the church prohibits masturbation?" When I relayed the question to the doctor, I avoided using the "m" word and simply asked, "How do you get sperm?"

Dr. McNally replied, "Ms. Doolittle, if your mother hasn't already explained that to you, I'm not sure I can help."

Dr. McNally remembered me when, a few months later, I phoned him again, and he consented to join my trivia team.

The week before the contest, I'd rented an antique black-sequined dress for an upcoming Halloween party at a haunted Hudson River mansion. Since I couldn't alter the dress's ample bust line, I bought a pair of those silicone breast forms that "increase your bust by two bra cup sizes."

The night of the trivia contest, I decided in the parking lot to put the breast forms to the test—to actually wear them and see if they stayed put. Sitting in my car, I scanned the area to make sure no one could see me and slipped them into place. Then off I went with those jelly-like forms wiggling under my red business suit.

Dr. McNally bought me a drink, and the contest began. I contributed little of value to our team, but toward the end of the evening, the God of Trivia threw me a bone with the following question: "Who wrote the poem that begins "The fog comes on little cat feet?'" No one knew the answer, not even the Good Doctor. But I did.

"Carl Sandburg" I said to the judges, ever so pleased with myself for clinching a bottle of wine for the team.

I went on to explain to anyone willing to listen how, when I was twelve-years-old, I wrote an essay about the poem, poking fun of the poet's metaphor in Mr. Kaye's English class at Scarsdale Junior High. Twenty-seven years later, that essay really paid off.

Ten months later, after that fateful night of trivia, Richard and I were married on Nantucket Island, despite my misleading him with those silicone forms.

And in case you're still wondering how the Catholic hospital obtained sperm specimens, it turned out there was a loophole. Although the medical laboratory was located in the hospital, it wasn't actually owned by the hospital per se, enabling the patients to "m" as much as they liked without fear of going blind.

ANNA PARET

Anna Geraldine Paret first came to New York as an investment banker transferred from London. She's lived in America for over twenty years—in Palo Alto, California, Washington, DC, and New York City. Anna and her husband currently live in Larchmont, New York; their oldest daughter attends university in England, and their youngest in Washington, DC. A former docent at Jasper Ridge Biological Preserve at Stanford University, Anna is presently a naturalist at Sheldrake Environmental Center in Larchmont. Her work has appeared in *Orbis #173, Inscape*—where she received the Editors Choice award for the poem, *What is the Grass?*—and *Ghost Town Literary Magazine*. She is a 2016 Scott Meyer Award short story finalist.

THE GREENEST SHADE OF GREEN
Anna Paret

The brunette Realtor in ballet flats pointed out, with a barely-perceptible straightening of her shoulders, that the majority of Larchmont homeowners are very well-educated and (therefore) that the schools here are marvelous. Certainly in the Great Outdoors beyond my frontdoor, in my neighborhood known locally as The Woods, it seems that every other housewife has a master's degree; every third, a Ph.D.

Rachel (M.Sc.) ran a Fortune 500 company before she ran the PTA. The mower-and blower who tends her garden was the first member of his family to graduate middle school. Rachel instructs him, with a bestowing sweep of her arm, to program her sprinkler system. Perhaps she can figure out how to telephone him when it's raining so that he can come and switch it off.

To be fair, Rachel's yard is perfect, her grass the greenest shade of green. I heard—I suspect I was supposed to hear—her telling Mr. Travis Next Door how to get rid of crabgrass and clover. It is unfortunate that Rachel has such a perfect view of my garden from her house.

Mr. Travis Next Door has a couple of sons in high school. We hear them. Sometimes they're loud and late, but they're in high school. Rachel said to me, "Those boys are out of control. And Mr. Travis is too much of a pushover. He should say something to them."

I thought, "Didn't you ever do anything stupid in high school, you self-righteous cow? I bet you did because everyone does, not only Mr. Travis Next Door's kids."

Rachel continued, "Mr. Travis should stop being a friend to those boys and start being their role model."

I said—quietly, "We're not there yet, Rachel." Rachel and I both have kids in middle school. In middle school, with the mower-and-blower's son.

Rachel has a cat. Mr. Travis Next Door has a dog. I heard—I'm pretty sure I was supposed to hear—Rachel telling Mr. Travis Next Door that he should make sure that his dog doesn't bark before ten a.m. because her twelve year old really needs to sleep in on a Saturday. ("We're thinking about Harvard.") Mr. Travis Next Door said, "Please keep your cat indoors. It's killing the birds in my yard."

I thought, "Way to go, Mr. Travis Next Door."

Next: Rachel's son (the Harvard prospect in sixth grade with the long, greasy bangs) took up the electric guitar. I heard Mr. Travis Next Door say to Rachel, "Please ask your son not to play the guitar after nine p.m. My dog really needs his sleep."

So when I walk my dog in the rain (a dog's got to do what a dog's got to do) and Rachel's sprinklers go off, catching me below the umbrella, and I feel a rumble of irritation like the tiny bubbles that skim across the bottom of a pan of water before it erupts in a boil, I offer up a silent prayer to Mr. Travis Next Door, then lob a loaded poo bag onto the greenest grass in The Woods.

LESSONS LEARNED

STEVEN LEWIS

Steven Lewis, Literary Ombudsman for *Read650*, is a columnist at *Talking Writing,* and a member of the Sarah Lawrence College Writing Institute faculty. A longtime freelancer, his work has been featured in the *New York Times, the Washington Post, Christian Science Monitor,* the *Los Angeles Times, Ploughshares, Spirituality & Health,* and other publications. His novels include *A Hard Rain, Take This and Loving Violet,* all from Codhill Press. Finishing Line Press published Steve's poetry chapbook, *If I Die Before You Wake.* His backlist includes *Zen and the Art of Fatherhood, The ABCs of Real Family Values, The Complete Guide for the Anxious Groom,* and *Fear and Loathing of Boca Raton (a Hippie's Guide to the New Sixties).* He divides his time between his writing space in New Paltz, New York and Hatteras Island, North Carolina.

NOT MY FATHER'S CADILLAC
Steven Lewis

My father was born in Brooklyn in 1908 and, like so many kids from those immigrant streets, pushed, bulled, and bullied his way through the rough crowds and, as they said back then, made something of himself.

The making did not come without cost, though. In the rubble of the Depression he gave up his dream of practicing law; and down that economic highway he came to an elemental fork: Go left and be a model dad like Ward Cleaver; go right, build a business, and leave the raising of kids to his wife. So, six days a week my father left the house before everyone was awake and twelve hours later came home long after the family had eaten and disappeared behind bedroom doors. Sundays he did paperwork. The man was so industrious, so single-minded, that he missed out on every soccer, baseball, and basketball game I played at Wheatley High. Never went to Ebbets Field. Never took me fishing.

That said, the great sacrifices my old man made did not come without some reward. Applying shoulder to wheel, he made a small business big enough to buy a ranch house on suburban Candy Lane (yes, Candy Lane). And a few years later traded the dependable

Buick for his dreamboat, a 1956 Cadillac Coupe de Ville.

My old man stood next to that powder blue beauty with a driveway-wide grin. His brothers, Murray (Hawaiian shirts) and Mac (argyle kneesocks), who also made somethings of themselves, drove Chrysler Imperials. There was no contest.

I was pleased as punch for my dad, at least until I began to wonder if it was possible he liked the Caddy more than me. And during the reign of the second Coupe de Ville, the '59 with the big gaudy fins, I finally bellowed out all my adolescent confusion and frustration, pointing right at the behemoth in the garage.

He had no idea what I was ranting about.

So in 1968, when Patti got pregnant and Dad was just settling into Cadillac number five, I righteously vowed never to put money or career before family. . . I would be a good dad. A great dad. If God Himself had pulled an Abraham on me, I would gladly submit to plague, pestilence, and Plymouths before I sacrificed my child . . . or owned a Cadillac.

So, you know where this is going . . . but let me drive you there my own route. I went on to lead the life I threatened I would. Went to every game, every concert, every ceremony, standing proudly next to my seven kids just as he stood beaming beside his Cadillacs. And from the driver's seat of a long succession of VW Vans and other clunky counter-culture cars full of stickers and dents and the spills of seven children, I found myself driving a rusty Honda Passport that whined and grunted and practically begged me to put it down.

Which was when, as these things happen in the karmic circle of life, my wife got a call from her father who had recently bought a Cadillac SRX and hated driving it. He offered it to us. For free!

Thus caught in the one-way traffic jam of my own making, I bellowed, "No! Look at me. I'm a beach dog! I'm a hipster! I have a f---ing ponytail!"

She looked at me like I was nuts. Like my late father would have looked at me.

She was right, of course.

So there I was all those incarnations later, Samuel Lewis' angry boy, all grown up and commandeering that Capitalist Pigmobile down Main Street in our funky upstate town, enduring endless razzing from friends and foes—and, what's worse, enjoying driving that lavish beast.

And for the first time gaining an appreciation for my father's pleasures . . . and the cosmic-sized sacrifices that went into attaining them.

Eventually the novelty faded, though, and I traded down for something I could drive on a beach. But when I handed over the keys to the salivating Toyota salesman, I realized that while my father may not have been a model dad like Ward Cleaver, as a son I was one big, ungrateful pain in the ass.

EDWARD McCANN

Edward McCann is an award winning writer/producer and the founder and editor of *Read650*, celebrating the spoken word with live events in New York City and throughout the tri-state area. A feature writer for *MILIEU* and a longtime contributing editor to *Country Living*, Ed's writing has been published in many literary journals, anthologies, and national magazines, including *Better Homes & Gardens, Good Housekeeping, The Irish Echo, The Sun,* and others. His essay, "Pregnant Again," was selected for the anthology, *Listen To Your Mother,* published by Penguin, and he's recently completed a memoir about the search for his missing nephew. He lives and writes in a pastoral spot about eighty miles north of New York City, and is at work on a collection of essays about life in the Hudson Valley.

REQUIEM
Edward McCann

Crouched before a cold fireplace with a lit match in my hand, I touched the flame to some crumpled newspaper tucked beneath the kindling, and a small headline on an adjacent page caught my eye: "College and Community Chorale to Resume." On impulse, I rescued that page and smoothed it flat on the floor. The fire crackled and roared to life as I read about a student choral group at the local college that welcomed community members—no auditions required. Rehearsals for a spring performance of Mozart's Requiem were about to begin—a three-hour class meeting for the next fifteen Wednesday nights.

I couldn't possibly do that, I thought, yet I hesitated to return the paper to the fire. The same impulse made me flag my calendar for the first class.

Though I had once loved choral singing, I catalogued all the reasons why I should just forget about this: other than some Christmas caroling, I hadn't sung in a chorus or choir in thirty years; I'd hardly touched a keyboard or guitar or even read a piece of sheet music in nearly as long. Besides, my work schedule was too demanding and unpredictable for me to make all those rehearsals.

I was still thinking this that late winter Wednesday as I walked into the music department's Recital Hall. All was instantly familiar: the water fountain and bulletin board, the scent of floor wax, and the sounds from a distant rehearsal room: a solo piano, a woman singing scales.

Feeling like an imposter, I signed out a copy of the bound, eighty page score, took a seat in the bass section at the rear of the room, and greeted the men around me. I counted fifty singers in the room, equally split between students and gray hairs like me. While the last stragglers arrived I opened the score and began reading. I was nervous. My armpits were damp. But I calmed myself recalling my beloved elementary school music teacher, Mrs. Diane Jacobs, who taught me "Every Good Boy Does Fine."

The accompanist, a small, bald man, settled himself on the bench before the baby grand in the front of the room. The director managed a perfunctory greeting and directed us to a page somewhere in the middle of the score.

"Okay," he said, raising his hand, "Sopranos."

The pianist played, and the women up front sang as if they already knew the piece. Staring at the music, I struggled to orient myself, to follow along as the women sang.

"Now," the director said, looking toward us, "Basses."

The piano again, then the collective intake of breath around me, followed by the sound of men singing, a resonance I felt in my chest. All those notes looked like birdshot scattered on the page. Still wondering if I should really have sat with the tenors, I found my place and joined in. But when that line ended I couldn't find the next bass clef fast enough, and they went on without me.

I can't do this I thought after rehearsal, certain I wouldn't return.

I felt unaccountably angry, and it seemed to me I'd been angry every day for the six months since my brother George had died—prematurely and unnecessarily in my opinion—anger that had shielded me from the grief that lurked just beneath it.

But I did return, fourteen more times, clocking nearly fifty hours singing a four-hundred-year-old funeral mass in Latin; a piece of music that's now become part of my DNA. Throughout all those hours of rehearsal, I was grieving, and I was singing that requiem for my lost brother.

Those Wednesday night rehearsals had begun in the dark, but as winter receded, the days grew longer—and brighter.

The evening of the recital, finally on stage in tuxedos and gowns, we sang Mozart's masterwork beside a twenty-six piece orchestra, all of us joining to form a complex machine assembled just this one time to make an extraordinary and beautiful sound.

And then, before I knew it . . . it was spring.

LESSONS LEARNED

ACKNOWLEDGMENTS

In addition to the contributors to this volume, we thank **Mihai Grunfeld** of the Vassar Lifelong Learning Institute or inviting us to produce our "Life Lessons" spoken word event on a Vassar College stage. We're also grateful to **Merrilee Osterhoudt** of the Marist Center for Lifetime Study and **Tom Esposito** of the Bard Lifetime Learning Institute for their participation and support of the event. All three organizations share similar missions and goals, offering a broad range of courses and activities to adults who love learning.
lifelonglearning.vassar.edu
lli.bard.edu
marist.edu/professional-programs/center-lifetime-study

We're grateful for the financial support of The **Hudson Valley Federal Credit Union**, a community-based financial cooperative committed to strengthening the quality of life for its members, friends, families, and neighbors in the Hudson Valley. For over fifty years, it has been their mission to provide affordable products and convenient services to help customers succeed financially through every stage of life.
hvfcu.org

A very special thanks to **Sheila Gilday** of Gilday Creative for her invaluable help in assembling this volume on short notice. Gilday Creative is a digitally forward independent website and graphic design agency based in the Hudson Valley that crafts strategies and design experiences to make things better.
gildaycreative.com/

LESSONS LEARNED

650
WHERE WRITERS READ

Read650.com

Info @Read650.com
facebook.com/Read650

LESSONS LEARNED

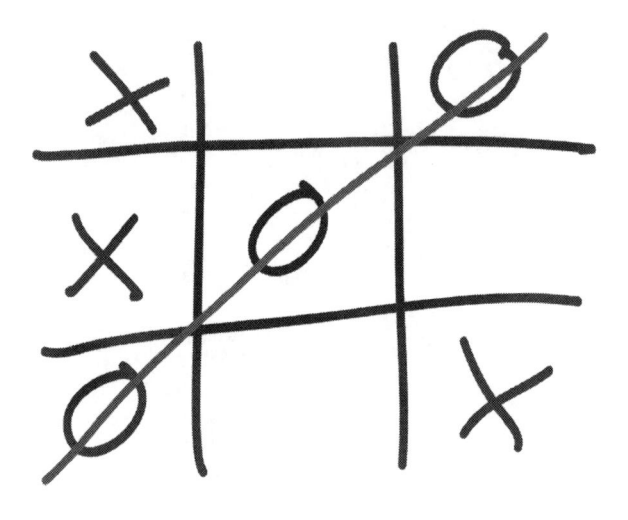

Made in the
USA
Lexington, KY